Comprehensive Aphasia Test

Kate Swinburn, Gillian Porter and David Howard

SCRIPT and
SCORING BOOKLET

CLIENT'S NAME: _____   DATE OF BIRTH: _____

ADMINISTRATOR'S NAME: _____   DATE: _____

Comprehensive Aphasia Test: Script and Scoring Booklet

(master score sheet at end of booklet)

Please read the Manual before administering the CAT and use the Manual in conjunction with this Scoring Booklet for both assessment and scoring.

Read aloud the text that is italicised. Follow all other instructions.

THE COGNITIVE SCREEN

1.   LINE BISECTION

GIVE THIS SCORING BOOK to the **person with aphasia** and turn to the next page (p. 2); rotate the book so that the lines are horizontal.

I want you to cut these lines in half like this, do you see the line is in two halves now? You try with this line.

Give AS MANY DEMONSTRATION items as you feel are necessary to establish comprehension of the task. Indicate to the person that you want him/her to do the same with the three lines on p. 5 WITHOUT POINTING directly to each test line (ensure they use a black or blue pen).

Here's your page. Can you cut all these lines in half?

Use the Line Bisection Scores Template on p. 5 (which could be photocopied onto an acetate for easier use) to determine scores.

Score line 1   . . . .

Score line 2   . . . .

Score line 3   . . . .

TOTAL   . . . .

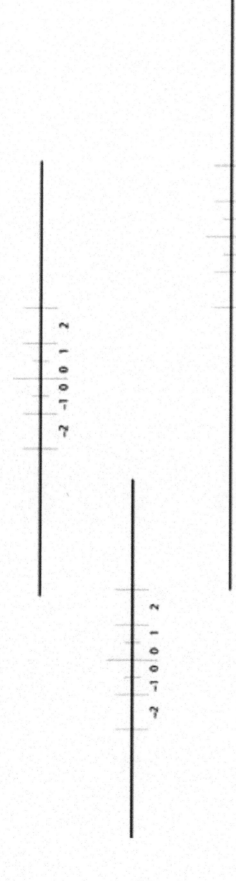

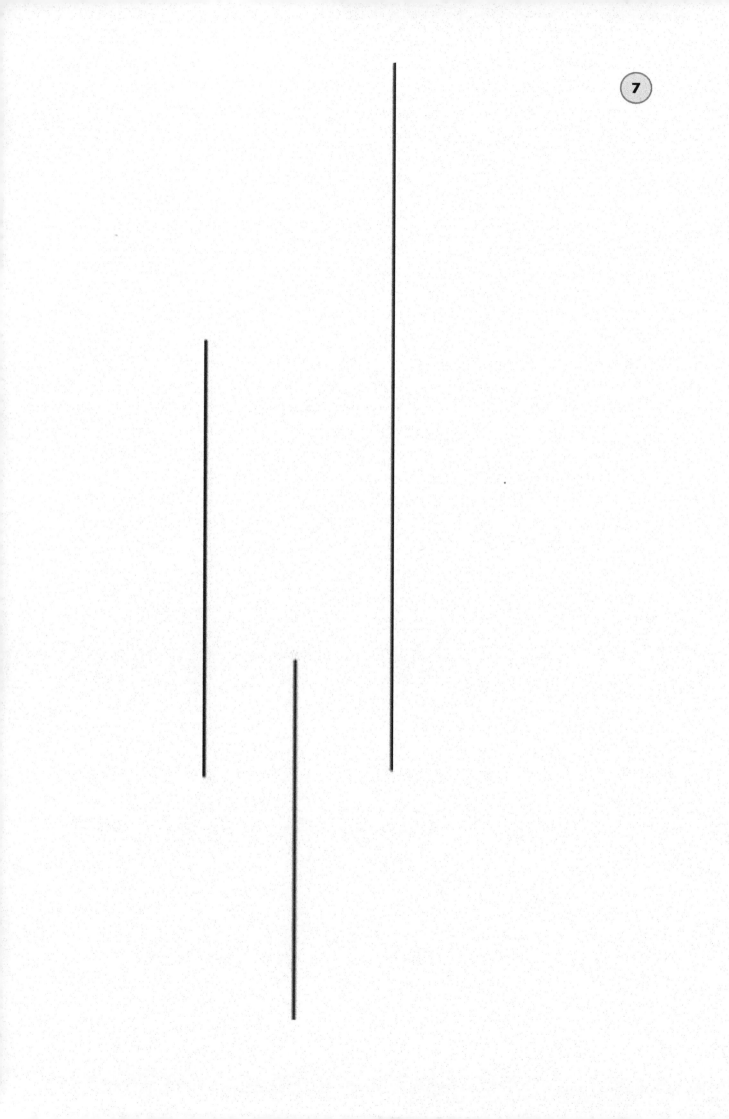

2.   SEMANTIC MEMORY (PP. 1–11 C&L)

You see we have a picture here [point to the monkey on p. 1 of the Cognitive & Language Test Book (C&L)] – *and one in each corner* [point to four picture choices]. *Which of these corner pictures goes best with this middle picture – which one is MOST ASSOCIATED?* (Gesture to aid comprehension.)

Show the practice item. This practice item can be done as often as needed. Proceed with the test items (give encouragement but not feedback).

	TARGET		CLOSE SEMANTIC DISTRACTOR		DISTANT SEMANTIC DISTRACTOR		UNRELATED DISTRACTOR	
P	banana	✓	pear		chocolate		envelope	
1	eye		ear		mouth		elephant	
2	mitten		sock		jersey		lighthouse	
3	candle		light bulb		radio		star	
4	bed		chair		stool		flag	
5	igloo		hut		house		sunshade	
6	arm		leg		neck		tortoise	
7	church		school		factory		skate	
8	fire		torch		rocket		picture	
9	clown		ballerina		priest		sheep	
10	watering can		bucket		shower		anchor	
Total		**/10**		**/10**		**/10**		**/10**

Leave a gap of approximately **three minutes** between the end of the "Semantic memory" and the beginning of the "Recognition memory" subtests. During this time, complete the "Word fluency" subtest.

3.   WORD FLUENCY (PP. 13–16 C&L)

I'm going to give you a minute.
Say out loud all the words that go in a category.
I'll give you an example . . . if I gave you the category "clothes" [point to written word on p. 13]
you might say . . . trousers, shirt, jumper, etc. . . . but your category isn't clothes, it's animals . . .
you've got to say as many animals as you can in a minute. (Repeat procedure for "s" words.)

For the practice item, show the word "clothes" and say some examples to demonstrate task requirements. Then show the written word "animals" in the C&L Test Book, say the word, and ask the person to name as many animals as possible. Write down responses in 15-second groupings. Then do the same with the letters. Demonstrate with the letter "b", and then ask the person to produce as many words as they can beginning with the letter "s" (p. 16). (If the person with aphasia supplies a proper noun, say "No names, please".)

TIME BAND	ANIMALS	"S"
0–15 seconds		
15–30 seconds		
30–45 seconds		
45–60 seconds		
No. of items named		

4.   RECOGNITION MEMORY (PP. 18–28 C&L)

One of these pictures you've seen before in this test [flick through previous pages without showing any of them specifically]. *Which one did you see before?*

P	TARGET		TOP LEFT	TOP RIGHT	BOTTOM LEFT	BOTTOM RIGHT
P	*monkey*		*scissors*	*foot*	*teapot*	***monkey***
1	glasses		shoe	**glasses**	table	piano
2	hand		soldier	frog	**hand**	axe
3	matches		nest	**matches**	bicycle	saw
4	pillow		pineapple	seahorse	**pillow**	kayak
5	Eskimo		racquet	basket	television	**Eskimo**
6	watch		tulip	**watch**	cot	wool
7	nun		**nun**	fish	tree	telephone
8	tent		**tent**	kite	castle	lifebelt
9	mask		nose	barber	**mask**	sailor
10	flower		cat	camel	fir tree	**flower**
	TOTAL		**/10**			

5. GESTURE OBJECT USE (PP. 30–36 C&L)

I want you to imagine I've put this object in your hand [gesture]. *SHOW ME what you do with it.*

Keep Test Book out of reach to encourage gesturing rather than pointing.

	TARGET	SCORE			MANNER OF RESPONSE*			COMMENT
P	pen	0	1	2	A	O	BPO	
1	peg	0	1	2	A	O	BPO	
2	comb	0	1	2	A	O	BPO	
3	mug	0	1	2	A	O	BPO	
4	scissors	0	1	2	A	O	BPO	
5	toothbrush	0	1	2	A	O	BPO	
6	paintbrush	0	1	2	A	O	BPO	
	TOTAL	**/12**						

* 2 = Gesture correct with no ambiguity
  1 = Action (A) or orientation (O) is incorrect, or if body part is used as object (BPO)
  0 = Incorrect

6. ARITHMETIC

Can you show me the answer to these sums please?
Go to next page (with arithmetic items).
Do **NOT** indicate the change of calculation type (e.g., addition/subtraction).
Ask the person to write in the correct answer or point to the correct answer to each sum (multiple choice). Underline the response.

Total = /6

[THIS IS THE END OF THE COGNITIVE SECTION]

9 + 6 =   (8   13   15   19   21)

7 − 4 =   (2   3   4   11   6)

8 × 7 =   (15   42   54   56   76)

14 + 18 =   (21   22   28   32   3)

34 − 15 =   (11   19   21   29   4)

147 + 58 =   (89   91   99   101   205)

Scoring system:

0 = incorrect

1 = correct after repetition of stimulus (R), self-correction (Sc) or significant delay (over 5 seconds) (D)

2 = correct with no assistance or delay

PART 1: LANGUAGE COMPREHENSION

7. COMPREHENSION OF SPOKEN WORDS (PP. 38–53 C&L)

I'm going to say a word.

I want you to point to the picture that goes best with that word.

Can you find me "mouse"? That's fine . . . there is always a picture that is close but not quite right [point to "mouse" and "rabbit"] . . . it's there to catch you out, so be careful.

TIME for 5 seconds. DISCONTINUE if the person makes four consecutive failures.

	TARGET	MANNER OF RESPONSE			SCORE			PHONOLOGICAL DISTRACTOR	NO. OF FEATURES DIFFERENT & POSITION		SEMANTIC DISTRACTOR	UNRELATED DISTRACTOR
P	*mouse*							*house*	*3df*	*I*	*rabbit*	*church*
1	ship	D	Sc	R	0	1	2	lip	2df	I	boat	nose
2	goat	D	Sc	R	0	1	2	coat	1df	I	sheep	dress
3	horn	D	Sc	R	0	1	2	horse	2df	F	trumpet	cow
4	boat	D	Sc	R	0	1	2	bone	2df	F	canoe	heart
5	dart	D	Sc	R	0	1	2	cart	2df	I	arrow	horse
6	knee	D	Sc	R	0	1	2	bee	2df	I	elbow	spider
7	pear	D	Sc	R	0	1	2	bear	1df	I	apple	lion
8	tyre	D	Sc	R	0	1	2	fire	2df	I	wheel	matches
9	leek	D	Sc	R	0	1	2	leaf	2df	F	carrot	flowers
10	kettle	D	Sc	R	0	1	2	kennel	2df	M	teapot	cage
11	hen	D	Sc	R	0	1	2	head	1df	F	cockerel	foot
12	roof	D	Sc	R	0	1	2	hoof	2df	I	chimney	tail
13	pine	D	Sc	R	0	1	2	pipe	3df	F	palm tree	cigarette
14	bull	D	Sc	R	0	1	2	wool	1df	I	cow	cotton
15	door	D	Sc	R	0	1	2	saw	2df	I	window	hammer
					(/15)	/30			/15		/15	/15

8. COMPREHENSION OF WRITTEN WORDS (PP. 55–70 C&L)

This is the same idea, only this time the word is written down for you there, I don't say anything.
So which picture goes with that word [point to the word "rocket"]?

TIME for 5 seconds. DISCONTINUE if the person makes four consecutive failures.

	TARGET	MANNER OF RESPONSE		SCORE			PHONOLOGICAL DISTRACTOR	NO. OF FEATURES DIFFERENT & POSITION		SEMANTIC DISTRACTOR	UNRELATED DISTRACTOR
P	rocket						pocket	3df	I	aeroplane	sleeve
1	mug	D	Sc	0	1	2	rug	2df	I	cup	carpet
2	pin	D	Sc	0	1	2	bin	1df	I	needle	basket
3	cap	D	Sc	0	1	2	cat	1df	F	hat	dog
4	nail	D	Sc	0	1	2	tail	2df	I	screw	leg
5	wall	D	Sc	0	1	2	ball	1df	I	fence	toys
6	boots	D	Sc	0	1	2	roots	2df	I	shoes	branches
7	pen	D	Sc	0	1	2	peg	2df	F	pencil	safety pin
8	rose	D	Sc	0	1	2	rope	3df	F	tulip	chain
9	bag	D	Sc	0	1	2	bat	2df	F	case	owl
10	boy	D	Sc	0	1	2	toy	2df	I	girl	dice
11	pig	D	Sc	0	1	2	wig	2df	I	cow	hat
12	lock	D	Sc	0	1	2	log	1df	I	key	tree
13	sun	D	Sc	0	1	2	nun	2df	I	moon	mayor
14	book	D	Sc	0	1	2	hook	3df	I	newspaper	noose
15	grass	D	Sc	0	1	2	glass	1df	M	flowers	bottle
				(/15)	/30		/15			/15	/15

9. COMPREHENSION OF SPOKEN SENTENCES (PP. 72–88 C&L)

*This is similar – only this time I say a **sentence** not a word. So you have to point to the picture that goes best with this sentence . . . ready?*

TIME for 5 seconds from the moment of saying the target sentence.

DISCONTINUE if the person makes four consecutive failures.

	SENTENCE TYPE[†]	TARGET SENTENCE	SELECTION	RESPONSE	SCORE
P	NP VP (1)	**A The woman is sitting** B The woman is *standing* C The *man* is *standing* D The *man* is sitting	**A** B C D	D Sc R	0 1 2
1	NP VP (1)	**B The woman is drinking** A The woman is *eating* C The *man* is drinking D The *man* is *eating*	A **B** C D	D Sc R	0 1 2
2	NP VP (1)	**C The man is walking** A The *woman* is *standing* B The *woman* is walking D The man is *standing*	A B **C** D	D Sc R	0 1 2
3	NP VP (1)	**C She is laughing** A *He* is laughing B She is *crying* D *He* is *crying*	A B **C** D	D Sc R	0 1 2
4	NP VP NP (2) I/A	**D The man is eating the apple** A The *woman* is eating the apple B The *woman* is eating an *ice-cream* C The man is eating an *ice-cream*	A B C **D**	D Sc R	0 1 2
5	NP VP NP (2) I/A	**B The woman is painting a wall** A The woman is painting a *picture* C The *man* is painting a *picture* D The *man* is painting a wall	A **B** C D	D Sc R	0 1 2
6	NP VP PP (2) I	**A The dog is sitting on the table** B The dog is sitting *under* the table C The *boy* is sitting on the table D The *boy* is sitting *under* the table	**A** B C D	D Sc R	0 1 2
7	NP VP NP (2) R	**B The apple is under the shoe** A The *pen* is under the *paper* C The *shoe* is under the *apple* D The *paper* is under the *pen*	A **B** C D	D Sc R	0 1 2

	SENTENCE TYPE[†]	TARGET SENTENCE	SELECTION			RESPONSE			SCORE		
8	NP VP NP	**B The nurse shoots the butcher**	A	**B**	C D	D	Sc	R	0	1	2
	(2)	A The *butcher* shoots the *nurse*									
	R/A	C The *butcher chases* the *nurse*									
		D The nurse *chases* the butcher									
9	NP VP NP	**C The singer hits the soldier**	A B	**C**	D	D	Sc	R	0	1	2
	(2)	A The singer *photographs* the soldier									
	R/A	B The *soldier photographs* the *singer*									
		D The *soldier* hits the *singer*									
10	NP VP PP	**A The policeman is painted by the dancer**	**A**	B	C D	D	Sc	R	0	1	2
	(2)	B The *dancer* is *chased* by the *policeman*									
	R/P	C The *dancer* is painted by the *policeman*									
		D The policeman is *chased* by the dancer									
11	NP VP PP	**D The butcher is chased by the nurse**	A B C	**D**		D	Sc	R	0	1	2
	(2)	A The *nurse* is *killed* by the *butcher*									
	R/P	B The butcher is *killed* by the nurse									
		C The *nurse* is chased by the *butcher*									
12	NP VP NP	**A The dancer paints the policeman**	**A**	B	C D	D	Sc	R	0	1	2
	(2)	B The *policeman chases* the *dancer*									
	R/A	C The *policeman* paints the *dancer*									
		D The dancer *chases* the policeman									
13	NP (*PP)	**D The shoe under the pencil is blue**	A B C	**D**		D	Sc	R	0	1	2
	VP NP	A (*shoe-under-pencil-blue*)**									
	(2)	B The shoe *on* the pencil is blue									
	R/E	C The *pencil* under the *shoe* is blue									
14	NP (*clause)	**A The carpet the cat is on is red**	**A**	B	C D	D	Sc	R	0	1	2
	VP NP	B The *red cat* is on the carpet									
	(2)	C/D Irrelevant									
	E										
15	NP VP PP	**C The red pencil is under the shoe**	A B	**C**	D	D	Sc	R	0	1	2
	(2)	A The red pencil is *on* the shoe									
	R	B The *green* pencil is under the shoe									
		D The red *shoe* is under the *pencil*									
16	NP (*PP)	**D The flower in the cup is blue**	A B C	**D**		D	Sc	R	0	1	2
	VP NP	A The flower *under* the cup is blue									
		B The flower *under* the cup is *green*									
		C (*flower-in-cup-blue*)**									
	TOTAL							(/16)		/32	

[†]Key: A = active sentence; P = passive sentence; R = reversible sentence; I = irreversible sentence; E = embedded sentence; ( ) = number of predicates; * = post-modifying; ** = using word order alone to comprehend this sentence

10. COMPREHENSION OF WRITTEN SENTENCES (PP. 90–106 C&L)

This time the sentences are written for you here – I don't say anything. When you're ready, point to the picture that goes with that sentence [point to the written sentence].

TIME for 5 seconds from when you've read the sentence to yourself.
DISCONTINUE if the person makes four consecutive failures.

	SENTENCE TYPE†	TARGET SENTENCE	SELECTION	RESPONSE	SCORE		
P	NP VP (1)	**D The man is sitting** A The *woman* is sitting B The *woman* is *standing* C The man is *standing*	A B C **D**	D Sc	0	1	2
1	NP VP (1)	**C The man is drinking** A The *woman* is *eating* B The *woman* is drinking D The man is *eating*	A B **C** D	D Sc	0	1	2
2	NP VP (1)	**B The woman is walking** A The woman is *standing* C The *man* is walking D The *man* is *standing*	A **B** C D	D Sc	0	1	2
3	NP VP (1)	**D He is crying** A He is *laughing* B *She* is crying C *She* is *laughing*	A B C **D**	D Sc	0	1	2
4	NP VP NP (2) I/A	**B The woman is eating an ice-cream** A The woman is eating an *apple* C The *man* is eating an ice-cream D The *man* is eating an *apple*	A **B** C D	D Sc	0	1	2
5	NP VP NP (2) I/A	**C The man is painting a picture** A The *woman* is painting a picture B The *woman* is painting a *wall* D The man is painting a *wall*	A B **C** D	D Sc	0	1	2
6	NP VP PP (2) I	**D The boy is sitting under the table** A The *dog* is sitting *on* the table B The *dog* is sitting under the table C The boy is sitting *on* the table	A B C **D**	D Sc	0	1	2
7	NP VP NP (2) R	**A The pen is under the paper** B The *apple* is under the *shoe* C The *shoe* is under the *apple* D The *paper* is under the *pen*	**A** B C D	D Sc	0	1	2

	SENTENCE TYPE†	TARGET SENTENCE	SELECTION				RESPONSE		SCORE		
8	NP VP NP (2) R/A	**A The butcher shoots the nurse** B The *nurse* shoots the *butcher* C The butcher *chases* the nurse D The *nurse chases* the *butcher*	**A**	B	C	D	D	Sc	0	1	2
9	NP VP NP (2) R/A	**D The soldier hits the singer** A The *singer photographs* the *soldier* B The soldier *photographs* the singer C The *singer* hits the *soldier*	A	B	C	**D**	D	Sc	0	1	2
10	NP VP PP (2) R/P	**C The dancer is painted by the policeman** A The *policeman* is painted by the *dancer* B The dancer is *chased* by the policeman D The *policeman* is *chased* by the *dancer*	A	B	**C**	D	D	Sc	0	1	2
11	NP VP PP (2) R/P	**C The nurse is chased by the butcher** A The nurse is *killed* by the butcher B The *butcher* is *killed* by the *nurse* D The *butcher* is chased by the *nurse*	A	B	**C**	D	D	Sc	0	1	2
12	NP VP NP (2) R/A	**C The policeman paints the dancer** A The *dancer* paints the *policeman* B The policeman *chases* the dancer D The *dancer chases* the *policeman*	A	B	**C**	D	D	Sc	0	1	2
13	NP (*PP) VP NP (2) R/E	**D The shoe under the pencil is red** A (*shoe-under-pencil-red*)** B The *pencil* under the *shoe* is red C The shoe *on* the pencil is red	A	B	C	**D**	D	Sc	0	1	2
14	NP (*clause) VP NP (2) R/E	**B The carpet the cat is on is green** C The *green cat* is on the carpet A/D Irrelevant	A	**B**	C	D	D	Sc	0	1	2
15	NP VP PP (2) R	**A The blue shoe is under the pencil** B The blue *pencil* is under the *shoe* C The blue shoe is *on* the pencil D The *red* shoe is under the pencil	**A**	B	C	D	D	Sc	0	1	2
16	NP (*PP) VP NP R	**B The flower under the cup is red** A (*flower-under-cup-red*)** C The flower *in* the cup is red D The *cup* under the *flower* is red	A	**B**	C	D	D	Sc	0	1	2
	TOTAL										**/32**

†Key: A = active sentence; P = passive sentence; R = reversible sentence; I = irreversible sentence; E = embedded sentence; ( ) = number of predicates; * = post-modifying; ** = using word order alone to comprehend this sentence

11. COMPREHENSION OF SPOKEN PARAGRAPHS
(P. 108 C&L)

I'm going to read you a short story. I want you to listen and then answer some questions. You should only say yes or no [point to yes/no on p. 108 C&L]. Are you ready?

Sally and Richard had been on the train for over three hours. They were tired and fed up. The train was already 45 minutes late, the buffet had closed so there was no food, and the lady opposite was snoring.

a.	Were Sally and Richard travelling by car?	Yes/**No**
b.	Were they on time?	Yes/**No**
a.	Were they travelling by train?	**Yes**/No
b.	Were they early?	Yes/**No** /2

OK – here's another one. Are you ready?

The explosion in central London caused havoc. Initially terrorists were suspected but it turned out not to be a bomb. The cause was found to be a burst gas main that ignited when someone had thrown down a lighted cigarette. People three miles away heard the explosion and the damage is estimated at over a million pounds.

a.	Was the explosion in Leicester?	Yes/**No**
b.	Was it caused by a bomb?	Yes/**No**
a.	Was it in London?	**Yes**/No
b.	Was the explosion caused by a gas main?	**Yes**/No /2

TOTAL CORRECT   /4

[THIS IS THE END OF THE LANGUAGE COMPREHENSION SECTION]

PART 2: EXPRESSIVE LANGUAGE

12. REPETITION OF WORDS

I'm going to say some words and I'd like you just to repeat them back to me.
   Ready? (Read the target words from the table below.)

	TARGET	IMAG		FREQ		LENGTH (SYLLABLES)		RESPONSE	MANNER OF RESPONSE	SCORE
P	table									
1	vine	H			L	1			D Sc R	0 1 2
2	president	H		H			3		D Sc R	0 1 2
3	scorn		L		L	1			D Sc R	0 1 2
4	radio	H		H			3		D Sc R	0 1 2
5	crucifix	H			L		3		D Sc R	0 1 2
6	trade		L	H		1			D Sc R	0 1 2
7	etiquette		L		L		3		D Sc R	0 1 2
8	plant	H		H		1			D Sc R	0 1 2
9	tomato	H			L		3		D Sc R	0 1 2
10	character		L	H			3		D Sc R	0 1 2
11	gilt		L		L	1			D Sc R	0 1 2
12	gravity		L		L		3		D Sc R	0 1 2
13	swamp	H			L	1			D Sc R	0 1 2
14	evidence		L	H			3		D Sc R	0 1 2
15	face	H		H		1			D Sc R	0 1 2
16	mind		L	H		1			D Sc R	0 1 2
		/8	/8	/8	/8	/8	/8		**TOTAL (/16)**	**/32**

Key: IMAG = imageability; FREQ = frequency; H = high; L = low

13. REPETITION OF COMPLEX WORDS

Continue reading the target words from the table below.

	TARGET	RESPONSE	MANNER OF RESPONSE	SCORE
1	unthinkable		D Sc R	0 1 2
2	defrosted		D Sc R	0 1 2
3	conforming		D Sc R	0 1 2
			TOTAL (/3)	**/6**

14.   REPETITION OF NONWORDS

*Now there are some nonsense words, made-up words. If you find yourself saying a real word you've got it wrong. **All** these words are nonsense.*

Read the target words from the table below.

	TARGET	RESPONSE	MANNER OF RESPONSE	SCORE
1	gart		D Sc R	0 1 2
2	clup		D Sc R	0 1 2
3	spenk		D Sc R	0 1 2
4	trimpy		D Sc R	0 1 2
5	prastode		D Sc R	0 1 2
			TOTAL (/5)	/10

15.   REPETITION OF DIGIT STRINGS

Now I'm going to say a string of numbers starting with two numbers and working up. So can you repeat these number strings? Ready?

Read out the FIRST LINE of each level. If the response is CORRECT, move on to the first line of the next level. If the response is INCORRECT, read out the second line of that level.

LEVEL	STIMULUS	RESPONSE (phonemic/dyspraxic errors ARE accepted)
2 items	7 2 1 3	
3 items	6 3 5 2 9 8	
4 items	4 5 2 7 5 6 9 1	
5 items	6 2 9 7 5 7 6 8 1 3	
6 items	7 8 4 1 6 9 3 6 8 2 9 4	
7 items	2 8 7 4 5 1 2 7 2 8 6 4 5 3	
	To obtain score, double the maximum length repeated correctly	(DIGIT SPAN 2 3 4 5 6 7) **TOTAL SCORE** /14

16. REPETITION OF SENTENCES

Now I'm going to say a sentence. Can you repeat each word that I've said? Ready?

Read out the FIRST SENTENCE of each level. If the person with aphasia repeats it CORRECTLY, move to the next level. If he/she FAILS, asks him/her to repeat the SECOND SENTENCE of that level. Write the response verbatim here.

No. CONTENT WORDS		STIMULUS (phonemic and obviously dyspraxic errors ARE accepted)
3 (5)		The **cat chased** the **bird**
	Response:	
		The **girl eats** the **apple**
	Response:	
4 (7)		The **man went** and **shut** the **window**
	Response:	
		They **decided** to **paint** the **room blue**
	Response:	
5 (9)		The **children listened** as the **teacher read** the **story**
	Response:	
		The **local map** was **small** and **difficult** to **read**
	Response:	
6 (11)		The **boy** and **girl climbed** the **hill** and **admired** the **view**
	Response:	
		It was a **long time before** the **area** was **pronounced safe**
	Response:	
		(SENTENCE SPAN 3 4 5 6) To obtain score, double the maximum length repeated correctly **TOTAL SCORE** /12

(Number in brackets refers to total number of words)

17. NAMING OBJECTS (PP. 110–134 C&L)

What's that a picture of?

If the person with aphasia is unable to name a picture, or names it incorrectly, provide a PHONEMIC CUE. If visual misperception of the picture is suspected, provide a SEMANTIC CUE. DISCONTINUE if there are eight consecutive failures.

See Manual for scoring details.

	TARGET	FREQ		IMAG		LENGTH (SYLLABLES)		RESPONSE (TRANSCRIPTION)	MANNER OF RESPONSE		SCORE		
P	car	H		H		1							
1	knife	H		H		1			D	Sc	0	1	2
2	star	H		H		1			D	Sc	0	1	2
3	spoon		LIn		L	1			D	Sc	0	1	2
4	cigarette	H		H		3			D	Sc	0	1	2
5	fox		LAn	H		1			D	Sc	0	1	2
6	aerial		LIn		L	3			D	Sc	0	1	2
7	pyramid		LIn	H		3			D	Sc	0	1	2
8	saxophone		LIn	H		3			D	Sc	0	1	2
9	pineapple		LAn		L	3			D	Sc	0	1	2
10	brush	H			L	1			D	Sc	0	1	2
11	telephone	H		H		3			D	Sc	0	1	2
12	crab		LAn		L	1			D	Sc	0	1	2
13	elephant		LAn	H		3			D	Sc	0	1	2
14	camera	H			L	3			D	Sc	0	1	2
15	frog		LAn	H		1			D	Sc	0	1	2
16	snail		LAn		L	1			D	Sc	0	1	2
17	caravan		LIn		L	3			D	Sc	0	1	2
18	drum		LIn	H		1			D	Sc	0	1	2
19	gate	H			L	1			D	Sc	0	1	2
20	crocodile		LAn		L	3			D	Sc	0	1	2
21	ski		LIn	H		1			D	Sc	0	1	2
22	butterfly		LAn	H		3			D	Sc	0	1	2
23	sock		LIn		L	1			D	Sc	0	1	2
24	envelope	H			L	3			D	Sc	0	1	2
		/8	/16	/12	/12	/12	/12	**TOTAL SCORE**	(	/24)			/48

Key: IMAG = imageability; FREQ = frequency; H = high; L = low; An = animate; In = inanimate

18. NAMING ACTIONS (PP. 136–141 C&L)

[Point to the picture of a man eating.] *What's that person **doing**?*

   TIME each response and transcribe each one in full.

	TARGET	RESPONSE (TRANSCRIPTION)	MANNER OF RESPONSE		SCORE	
P	*eating*					
1	winding		D	Sc	0 1 2	
2	sawing		D	Sc	0 1 2	
3	threading		D	Sc	0 1 2	
4	typing		D	Sc	0 1 2	
5	licking		D	Sc	0 1 2	
			TOTAL SCORE	(/5)	/10	

19.   SPOKEN PICTURE DESCRIPTION (P. 143 C&L)

Tell me what's happening in this picture.

If the person misses out areas of the picture, point to them and ask "what about that?" or some such prompt.

TRANSCRIBE their response in the space below.

See Manual for scoring, and Appendix 1 for worked examples.

A APPROPRIATE ICWS	B INAPPROPRIATE ICWS	C SYNTACTIC VARIETY	D GRAMMATICAL WELL-FORMEDNESS	E SPEED
A Total =	**B Total =**	**C Total =**	**D Total =**	**E Total =**

Key: ICWS = information-carrying words

TOTAL SCORE (A − B) + C + D + E =

20.   READING WORDS (P. 145 C&L)

Here are some words. Could you read them out aloud for me?

Cover the preceding words with card if helpful.

	TARGET	FREQ		IMAG		REG		SYLL	RESPONSE	MANNER OF RESPONSE		SCORE		
P	*chair*													
1	worm		L	H			I			D	Sc	0	1	2
2	fraud		L		L	R				D	Sc	0	1	2
3	yacht		L	H			I			D	Sc	0	1	2
4	hand	H		H		R				D	Sc	0	1	2
5	dynasty		L		L			3		D	Sc	0	1	2
6	horse	H		H		R				D	Sc	0	1	2
7	tomato		L	H				3		D	Sc	0	1	2
8	trout		L	H		R				D	Sc	0	1	2
9	break	H			L		I			D	Sc	0	1	2
10	vest		L	H		R				D	Sc	0	1	2
11	cause	H			L	R				D	Sc	0	1	2
12	family	H		H				3		D	Sc	0	1	2
13	side	H			L	R				D	Sc	0	1	2
14	position	H			L			3		D	Sc	0	1	2
15	give	H			L		I			D	Sc	0	1	2
16	cathedral		L	H				3		D	Sc	0	1	2
17	plead		L		L	R				D	Sc	0	1	2
18	century	H			L			3		D	Sc	0	1	2
19	head	H		H			I			D	Sc	0	1	2
20	hospital	H		H				3		D	Sc	0	1	2
21	shone		L		L		I			D	Sc	0	1	2
22	ridicule		L		L			3		D	Sc	0	1	2
23	dread		L		L		I			D	Sc	0	1	2
24	blood	H		H			I			D	Sc	0	1	2
	N	/12	/12	/12	/12	/8	/8	/8	**TOTAL SCORE**	(	/24)		/48	

Length: 1 syllable (reg + irreg scores)   =   /16

3 syllable   =   /8

Key: FREQ = frequency; IMAG = imageability; REG = regularity of spelling – sound; SYLL = syllables; H = high; L = low; R = regular; I = irregular

REMAINDER OF TARGET WORDS ("INFORMATIVE" . . . "JIDDER") ARE SCORED ON THE FOLLOWING PAGES

21. READING COMPLEX WORDS (P. 145 C&L)

	TARGET	RESPONSE	MANNER OF RESPONSE		SCORE		
1	informative		D	Sc	0	1	2
2	recooked		D	Sc	0	1	2
3	presenting		D	Sc	0	1	2
		TOTAL SCORE					**/6**

22. READING FUNCTION WORDS (P. 145 C&L)

	TARGET	RESPONSE	MANNER OF RESPONSE		SCORE		
1	but		D	Sc	0	1	2
2	of		D	Sc	0	1	2
3	and		D	Sc	0	1	2
		TOTAL SCORE					**/6**

23. READING NONWORDS (P. 145 C&L)

Now these are all nonsense words. Have a go at reading those aloud.

	TARGET	RESPONSE	MANNER OF RESPONSE		SCORE		
1	fask		D	Sc	0	1	2
2	tib		D	Sc	0	1	2
3	thirk		D	Sc	0	1	2
4	deggle		D	Sc	0	1	2
5	jidder		D	Sc	0	1	2
		TOTAL SCORE					**/6**

WRITING (SUBTESTS 24–27)

See the C&L Test Book for instructions (pp. 146–156).

Read instructions from the guide in the **Test Book**.

Give this **Scoring Book** to the **person with aphasia**.

Score the results **later**. (Score sheets appear on pp. 33-34 of this book.)

Please write your name

_____

Please write these ALL in CAPITALS

T   C   H   A   Y

_____

(practice)

d   e   r   b   f   g

_____

cup   feet   toothbrush

_____   _____   _____

Please write the names of these pictures:

P. _____

1. _____

2. _____

3. _____

4. _____

5. _____

Please listen and write these words:

P. _____

1. _____

2. _____

3. _____

4. _____

5. _____

What is happening in this picture?

24. WRITING: COPYING (P. 146 C&L)

	Letters written correctly
Copying – same case – letters	/5
Copying – cross case – letters	/5
Copying – cross case – words	/17
TOTAL SCORE	**/27**

25. WRITING PICTURE NAMES (PP. 147–153 C&L)

Disregard case.

Score letters not words (see Manual for example).

(✓) Correct letter, correct position relative to adjacent letters. Score 1

(S) Substitution   Score 0

(O) Omission   Score 0

(T) Transposition   Score 0

Transposition of two adjacent letters is counted as a single error (score 0 for first letter, +1 no penalty for second letter).

(A) Additional letters   Score − 1 from the **total** score

(regardless of how many additional letters)

(SP) Semantically related verbal paraphasias are scored as 0

	TARGET	WORD TYPE	RESPONSE	TYPE OF RESPONSE (✓, S, O, T, A, SP)	LETTER SCORING (+1, 0, −1)	SCORE
P	hat	HiF, HiI, Reg				
1	boy	HiF, HiI, Reg				/3
2	eye	HiF, HiI, Irreg				/3
3	pear	LoF, HiI, Reg (with homophone possibility)				/4
4	tank	LoF, HiI, Reg				/4
5	giraffe	LoF, HiI, Irreg				/7
					TOTAL SCORE	**/21**

Key: F = frequency; I = imageability; Hi = high; Lo = low; Reg = regular; Irreg = irregular

26. WRITING TO DICTATION (P. 154 C&L)

Disregard case.

	TARGET	WORD TYPE	RESPONSE	TYPE OF RESPONSE (✓, S, O, T, A, SP)	LETTER SCORING (+1, 0, −1 see above)
P	*pen*	*HiF, HiI, Reg*			
1	man	HiF, HiI, Reg			/3
2	yacht	LoF, HiI, Irreg			/5
3	idea	LoF, LoI, Reg			/4
4	undrinkable	LoF, LoI, Reg, Morph complex			/11
5	blosh	nonword			/5
				TOTAL SCORE	**/28**

Key: F = frequency; I = imageability; Hi = high; Lo = low; Reg = regular; Irreg = irregular; Morph complex = morphologically complex

27. WRITTEN PICTURE DESCRIPTION (PP. 155–156 C&L)

A APPROPRIATE ICWS	B INAPPROPRIATE ICWS	C GRAMMATICAL WELL-FORMEDNESS
A Total =	**B Total =**	**C Total =**

TOTAL SCORE (A − B) + C =

[[THIS IS THE END OF THE LANGUAGE SECTION]]

PART 3: APHASIA IMPACT QUESTIONNAIRE

(Administrators should read aloud the italicised text and follow all other instructions.)

Read this script or, once familiar with the procedure, read the text directly from the AIQ itself.

How are you feeling today? Show 'How are you feeling' page.

If it's a negative response, check if the person wishes to carry on, delay or abandon the administration altogether.

*We're going to **talk** about **aphasia** today.* Aphasia is difficulty talking, understanding, reading and writing (point to the corresponding pictures).

*We're going to talk about **how aphasia affects life for you**. Does it affect **what you do** and **how you feel?***

*We're going to go through **this questionnaire**. The questions are **all** about how things have been **during the last week.***

*It is **your view** of how things are. There is **no right** or **wrong**.*

*Before we start, let's **choose a scale.***

*Which person **looks** most **like you?***

Person with aphasia selects appropriate image. You give the person the AIQ Rating Scale booklet showing that same image, to refer to throughout.

I'll show you a picture and ask a question (show Q1.). ***You** will use your scale* Point to the Scale chosen by the person with aphasia.

*I want you to think about **how things have been** in the **last week – overall** this last week.*

*Remember there is **no right or wrong answer**. It is **your** view of how things feel about **life with aphasia**, just during **this last week.***

*Let's start with a question about **you talking** to other people.*

NOW TURN TO QUESTION 1. OF THE QUESTIONNAIRE (This week ... how easy was it for you to **talk** to ...)

28. COMMUNICATION (PP. 4–10 AIQ)

So, we're looking at your talking – finding words and saying a sentence.
[Reveal p. XXX of AIQ, and so on.]
During the last week, how easy is it for you to:

1. talk to [use person's name] **the person closest to you?**
Present the 'This week, how easy was it to talk to [. . .] someone closest to you?' page.
NB – use the name of the person closest to them if you know it.
if talking to X was very easy, the same as before your stroke, point here (point to far right of the scale)
if you couldn't talk at all, impossible, you would point here (point to far left of the scale)
but maybe its somewhere in between (sweep hand across the scale).
So, what do you think – how easy was talking with XX . . . show me on the scale?
So, it can be any one of these (point to all five people on the scale)
can you show me on the scale? (sweep your hand across the whole scale).
Great. That's the idea.
Comments

Rating: 4 3 2 1 0

2. talk to someone you don't know, a stranger?
Prompt if needed: suggest " . . . someone like me", or " . . . someone in a shop."
Comments

Rating: 4 3 2 1 0

Now we are going to think about your **understanding** *. . . so someone else is talking, you must follow what they say . . . So, during the last week*

3. how easy was it to understand [use person's name] **someone close to you?**
Gesture and if needed, prompt: " . . . follow what is being said."
Comments

Rating: 4 3 2 1 0

4. We are still thinking about your **understanding** . . . in the last week, how easy was it to understand **someone you don't know?**   **Rating:**   4   3   2   1   0
Prompt if needed: "*a stranger.*"
Comments

5. During the last week, how easy was it for you to **write a message** to a **friend?**   **Rating:**   4   3   2   1   0
Prompt: "*. . . to* **find** *and* **spell** *the words*", "*. . . in a* **card**", "*. . . in an* **email.**"
Comments

When you do write, do you prefer to email, text or use pen and paper? **CIRCLE RESPONSE HERE**

6. During the last week, how easy was it for you to **read a news story?**   **Rating:**   4   3   2   1   0
Prompt: "*. . . from your* **phone**", "*. . . in an actual* **paper**", "*. . . on a* **computer**"
Comments

29.   PARTICIPATION (PP. 11–14 AIQ)

*Now we are going to look at **things you had to do** this week. Prompt: "chores"*
So overall, during the last week, if things you had to do were very easy, point here.
If things you had to do were very difficult, you would point here.

7. *First, how easy was it for you to do things you **had to do** this week, like . . . .*
Point to each **corresponding picture** as you identify . . . .
• *Appointments?*
• *Transport?*
• *Paperwork/Money?*
• *Shopping?*
So overall, how easy was it for you to do things you had to do this week?
Comments

Rating: 4   3   2   1   0

8. *Now what about **things** you **wanted to do** this week? Were you able to do **enough positive things** you wanted to do?*
Point to each **corresponding picture** as you identify . . . .
• *Going to groups or clubs?*
• *Holidays?*
• *Going out?*
• *Hobbies?*
*If you were able to do **lots of positive things to do**, point here.*
*If you **couldn't do any** positive things, you point here.*
Comments

Rating: 4   3   2   1   0

9. *Now we are going to think about your **friends** .*
*So, during the last week, **how** were **things** with your **friends?***
*If things with your **friends were very good** this week, point here.*
If things with your friends were very difficult, point here.
Comments

Rating: 4   3   2   1   0

10. *Now we are going to think about your **family** .*
(There are three diverse family groups. Use whichever group the person chooses.)
So, during the last week, how were things with your family?
*If **things** with your **family** were **very good** this week, point here.*
*If things with your family were **very difficult** , point here.*
Comments

Rating: 4   3   2   1   0

30. EMOTIONAL WELLBEING (PP. 15–25 AIQ)

Now there are some questions about how you've felt this week. We have talked to other people with aphasia. They told us how they feel sometimes.

Can we check if you share these feelings or not? Let's start with frustration.

Monitor the person's reactions closely. If they are struggling, ascertain if they wish to carry on.

---

11. So, this week, have you felt frustrated?
If you have felt very frustrated, you would point here.
If you have not felt at all frustrated, point here.
Or it could be somewhere in between.
Prompt: " . . . wound up"
Comments

Rating: 4 3 2 1 0

---

12. What about being worried, have you felt worried this week?
Prompt: " . . . anxious"
Comments

Rating: 4 3 2 1 0

---

13. During the last week, have you felt unhappy?
Prompt: " . . . sad"
Comments

Rating: 4 3 2 1 0

---

14. Some people have told us they feel helpless. Have you felt helpless this week?
Prompt: " . . . powerless"
Comments

Rating: 4 3 2 1 0

---

15. Have you felt bored?
Prompt: " . . . nothing interesting"
Comments

Rating: 4 3 2 1 0

16. *During the last week, have you felt* **embarrassed***?*
Prompt: *" . . . ashamed"*
Comments

Rating: 4 3 2 1 0

17. *Have you felt* **angry** *this week?*
Prompt: *" . . . cross"*
Comments

Rating: 4 3 2 1 0

18. *During the last week, have you felt* **isolated***?*
Prompt: *" . . . on your own/cut off"*
Comments

Rating: 4 3 2 1 0

19. *I* **know** *that you are* **not stupid***, but* **some people** *tell us they* **sometimes feel stupid***.*
During the **last week** *, have you felt* **stupid***?*
Prompt: *" . . . feeling daft"*
Note: Administrators can often feel uncomfortable asking this question, but it has been extensively researched with people with aphasia and they do not share the same misgivings. When specifically asked about this question, no-one has felt it should be removed. Instead, they report it was an important opportunity to discuss whether they do or don't *feel stupid.*
Comments

Rating: 4 3 2 1 0

20. *Do you feel* **confident***?*
Prompt: *" . . . assured"*
Comments

Rating: 4 3 2 1 0

21. *Now we are thinking about the* **future** *.*
During the last week, how have you felt about the future?
Prompt: *" . . . optimistic?"*
Comments

Rating: 4 3 2 1 0

'Enjoy?' page P. 26
*Are there things you **enjoy** doing these days?* **DO NOT RATE**
Prompt: *" . . . like to do?"*

Going for a drive	Being with family	Enjoying music
Gardening	Doing something creative e.g., drawing	Seeing a friend
Seeing lots of friends	Caring for a pet	A social club e.g., bowling, bingo, wine club
Going outside e.g., going for a walk	Something physical e.g., going for a swim	Being pampered e.g., having a haircut

'Anything else?' page
*Is there **anything else** you'd like to add about life with aphasia for you?*

Thank the person for completing the assessment.

If it feels appropriate, give a condensed summary of what the person has expressed, and if negative emotions have been expressed, confirm that now can be the hardest time, that you are there to help and that sharing their experiences and feeling will help plan therapy that works for them.

Ensure enough time for more relaxed conversation before finishing.

[[THIS IS THE END OF THE APHASIA IMPACT QUESTIONNAIRE]]

MASTER SCORE SHEET

Subtest/Section	TEST 1 Number Correct	TEST 1 Score	TEST 1 T-Score*	TEST 2 Number Correct	TEST 2 Score	TEST 2 T-Score*	TEST 3 Number Correct	TEST 3 Score	TEST 3 T-Score*	Cut-off Score
COGNITIVE SCREEN										
1. Line bisection										±2.5
2. Semantic memory TEST 1 TEST 2 TEST 3 Error types:** Close semantic /10 /10 /10 Distant semantic /10 /10 /10 Unrelated /10 /10 /10		/10			/10			/10		8/10
3. Word fluency TEST 1 TEST 2 TEST 3 Animals: "s": Total:										13
4. Recognition memory		/10			/10			/10		8/10
5. Gesture object use		/12			/12			/12		9/10
6. Arithmetic		/6			/6			/6		1/6
Cognitive TOTAL		**/38**			**/38**			**/38**		

LANGUAGE BATTERY

Part 1: Language comprehension (note order of subtests)

Subtest/Section	TEST 1			TEST 2			TEST 3			Cut-off Score
	Number Correct	Score	T-Score*	Number Correct	Score	T-Score*	Number Correct	Score	T-Score*	
Comprehension of spoken language										
7. Comprehension of spoken words Error types:** TEST 1 TEST 2 TEST 3 Phonological /15 /15 /15 Semantic /15 /15 /15 Unrelated /15 /15 /15	/15	/30		/15	/30		/15	/30		25/30
9. Comprehension of spoken sentences	/16	/32		/16	/32		/16	/32		27/32
11. Comprehension of spoken paragraphs		/4			/4			/4		2/4
Comprehension of spoken language TOTAL		**/66**			**/66**			**/66**		**56/66**
Comprehension of written language										
8. Comprehension of written words Error types:** TEST 1 TEST 2 TEST 3 Phonological /15 /15 /15 Semantic /15 /15 /15 Unrelated /15 /15 /15	/15	/30		/15	/30		/15	/30		27/30
10. Comprehension of written sentences	/16	/32		/16	/32		/16	/32		23/32
Comprehension of written language TOTAL		**/62**			**/62**			**/62**		**53/66**

Continued...

Part 2: Expressive language

Subtest/Section	TEST 1			TEST 2			TEST 3			Cut-off Score
	Number Correct	Score	T-Score*	Number Correct	Score	T-Score*	Number Correct	Score	T-Score*	
Repetition										
12. Repetition of words	/16	/32		/16	/32		/16	/32		29/32
13. Repetition of complex words	/3	/6		/3	/6		/3	/6		5/6
14. Repetition of nonwords	/5	/10		/5	/10		/5	/10		5/10
15. Repetition of digit strings	/14	/14		/14	/14		/14	/14		8/10 (span of 4)
16. Repetition of sentences	/12	/12		/12	/12		/12	/12		10/12 (span of 5)
Repetition TOTAL	**/50**	**/74**		**/50**	**/74**		**/50**	**/74**		**67/74**
Spoken language production										
17. Naming objects	/24	/48		/24	/48		/24	/48		43/48
Use of phonological cues										
18. Naming actions	/5	/10		/5	/10		/5	/10		8/10
Word fluency TOTAL (subtest 3 from COGNITIVE SCREEN)										
Naming TOTAL (sum objects/actions/fluency)										**69**
Spoken picture description										
19. Spoken picture description										33
Reading aloud										
20. Reading words	/24	/48		/24	/48		/24	/48		45/48
21. Reading complex words	/3	/6		/3	/6		/3	/6		4/6
22. Reading function words	/3	/6		/3	/6		/3	/6		3/6
23. Reading nonwords	/5	/10		/5	/10		/5	/10		6/10
Reading TOTAL	**/35**	**/70**		**/35**	**/70**		**/35**	**/70**		**58/70**

Subtest/Section	TEST 1			TEST 2			TEST 3			Cut-off Score
	Number Correct	Score	T-Score*	Number Correct	Score	T-Score*	Number Correct	Score	T-Score*	
Writing										
24. Writing: Copying		/27			/27			/27		25/27
25. Writing picture names		/21			/21			/21		15/21
26. Writing to dictation		/28			/28			/28		24/28
Writing TOTAL		**/76**			**/76**			**/76**		**66/76**
Written picture description										
27. Written picture description										19

Part 3: Aphasia Impact Questionnaire - Concise

	Number Correct	Score	T-Score*	Number Correct	Score	T-Score*	Number Correct	Score	T-Score*	Cut-off Score
28. Communication		/24			/24			/24		***
29. Participation		/16			/16			/16		***
30. Emotional well-being		/44			/44			/44		***
AIQ TOTAL		**/84**			**/84**			**/84**		***

Cognitive Screen subtests score 0/1, except "Gesture object use" (0/1/2).
Language Battery subtests score 0/1/2 (see p. 12 of this book for scoring instructions).
* Calculate T-scores from tables in Appendices 2–7.
** Error types are given for reference only and do not affect scores.
*** There are no cut-off scores for AIQ items, as the questionnaire was not attempted with people with non-aphasic language.

T-SCORE PROFILE TEMPLATE

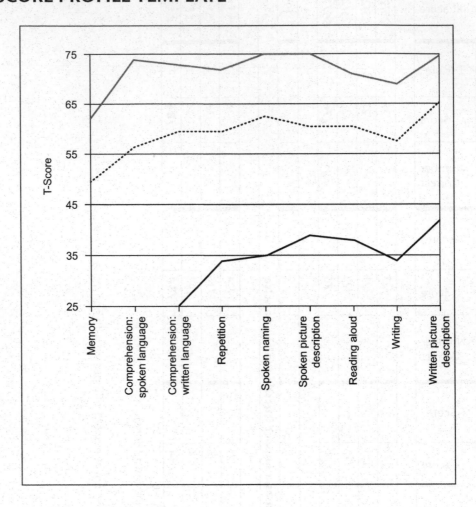